# Stop Smoking

How To Master Your Life And Overcome Nicotine
Dependence With Lasting Results

*(Finding The Method That Serves You Best)*

**Gabriel Haney**

# **TABLE OF CONTENT**

Tobacco Use And Your Health ................................. 1

Negative Effects Of Cigarette/Tobacco Emissions ........................................................ 14

Benefits Of Quitting ..................................... 23

Organizing Your Stop Smoking Plan ................... 28

Conclusion ................................................. 39

How To Stop Using - The Rapid Method ............ 40

How To Stop Smoking ................................. 82

Restating Mental Sobriety ........................... 87

Why You Ought To Stop Smoking .................... 115

# Tobacco Use And Your Health

The colossal increase in cigarette smoking during the 20th century has been the primary factor in the rise in the number of tobacco-related deaths and cases of disease. During this period, cigarette smoking grew to account for approximately 80% of the global tobacco market. In any event, all tobacco products are hazardous and addictive. In certain regions of the globe, the use of smokeless tobacco products poses a significant health risk.

Tobacco products are manufactured with a variety of additives to protect the tobacco's shelf life, alter its copying qualities, control its moisture content, prevent the hatching of insect eggs that may be present in the plant material, conceal the irritative effects of nicotine, and add a variety of flavors and fragrances. When tobacco and these additives are burned, the resulting vapor contains more than 4,000 synthetic compounds. Numerous of these mixtures are extremely toxic and have varying effects on health.

Nicotine, tar (the byproduct of combustion), and gases such as carbon dioxide and carbon monoxide are the primary components of tobacco smoke. Despite the fact that nicotine can be toxic in extremely high concentrations, its toxicity in tobacco smoke is generally considered to be negligible compared to that of numerous other toxins in the smoke. The primary effect of nicotine on health is its addictive nature. Carbon monoxide has significant and rapid health effects. It efficiently travels from the lungs to the circulatory system, where it binds to hemoglobin, the molecule in red platelets responsible for the exchange of oxygen within the body. Carbon monoxide displaces oxygen from the hemoglobin particle and is expelled gradually. Consequently, smokers frequently accumulate elevated levels of carbon monoxide, which deprives the body of oxygen and stresses the entire cardiovascular system.

The negative effects of smoking are not limited to the smoker alone. The harmful components of tobacco smoke are present not only in the smoke inhaled by the smoker, but also in environmental tobacco smoke, or passed-down cigarette smoke — that is, the smoke exhaled by the smoker (standard smoke) and the smoke that rises directly from the burning hot tobacco (sidestream smoke). Nonsmokers who are routinely exposed to environmental tobacco smoke are at an increased risk for some of the same diseases that plague smokers, such as cellular degeneration in the lungs and cardiovascular disease.

Prepare Yourself to Kick the Butt!

If you have reached the point where you are willing to quit smoking and give your health an opportunity to recover naturally, then congratulations, you have already won half the battle. More than fifty percent of smokers never reach this stage where they choose life over addiction. When you have this sensation in your heart, you know that momentum has been established. The journey will not be simple, but it will ultimately be filled with benefits and rewards.

You become physically, psychologically, and even behaviorally dependent on nicotine when you smoke. It is referred to as smoker's reflexes when one is profoundly aligned with a habit. It cannot be abandoned overnight, and a resolution for the new year will not suffice! To quit smoking, you must deprogram your entire system, analyze your behavior when cravings are unsatisfied, and implement the recommendations to correct that behavior. This is a lengthy and arduous process that calls for tremendous self-control and discipline. The most effective strategy to propel you forward is to:

- Postpone - Avoid - Substitute

Avoid Cigarettes

If only it were that simple! However, as obvious as it may seem, the fundamental principle of quitting rests in a single simple strategy: AVOID! The objective here is to modify your thinking and end your dependence. If possible, maintain a distance from smokers until you are no longer in control of your addiction. These suggestions will aid you in getting started.

- Don't take that cigarette break, do something else instead. - Learn to say no when you are offered to smoke. - Socialize more with non-smokers. - Cut down at least one cigarette per day. - Keep all visual cues such as lighter, cigarette, ashtray, etc. out of sight. - Avoid consuming alcohol, coffee, tea, and cola for as long as possible.

Plan your cessation date after your menstrual cycle if you are a woman, as withdrawal symptoms are more tolerable during this time.

Replace your Cigarettes with a Healthier Alternative

You have consistently conditioned your mind and body to rely on cigarettes for their feel-good effect over the years. It is going to be challenging to overcome. However, you can distract yourself from smoking by engaging in activities that you enjoy or are ardent about. Refrain from being anywhere near the location that triggers your craving. Until you are entirely deprogrammed, do not expose yourself to a tempting environment. Some of these suggestions may be useful!

Replace your smoking impulses with something more strenuous, such as sweat-inducing physical activities. Dance, walk, swim, exercise, or engage in any other form of movement that keeps you energized - Seek out other enjoyable activities such as music, acting, reading, etc.

- When feeling lonely, occupy your hands with objects such as a pencil, paper clip, or elastic band.

- You can also perform an instrument, work on a computer, be imaginative, or draw something.

Keeping your mouth occupied is another method for combating the urge. Chew a lozenge or cardamom. It is possible to clean your teeth multiple times per day.

Toothpaste makes cigarettes less pleasurable.

- Think positively and continue your voyage forward. If you can convince yourself to smoke, you can also persuade yourself not to smoke. It is all about perseverance and remaining true to your objective.

- Maintain composure and deep inhalation. You can also practice yoga or learn relaxation techniques such as meditation that will teach you to maintain mental control.

- Save the money you would typically spend on cigarettes and spend it on something more satisfying, such as a vacation, a new dress, or anything else!

Advice for combating this addiction

Essentially, quitting smoking is a five-step procedure. You are well on your way to becoming a nonsmoker if you can prepare yourself for your last cigarette and be prepared to deal with the cravings and withdrawals you will experience during this transition.

- Set a date by which you will resign and sign a contract.

Choose a date within the next week for quitting smoking. Use your close acquaintances and family members as witnesses to the contract's signing. Now, progressively prepare yourself mentally for the approaching date when you will quit smoking. Reduce the number of cigarettes you smoke daily until that date and increase your resolve to remain smoke-free.

- Choose one of these three strategies to cease smoking

oCold Turkey: This one is difficult, requires tremendous control, and may not be everyone's forte. When you reach your quit date, you cease smoking immediately and never look back. Once you are able to manage the withdrawal symptoms, it is rapid and grueling, but manageable.

oReduce the number of cigarettes you smoke each day. If you smoke 10 cigarettes per day, reduce the number by one each day until you reach your cessation date.

Count the number of draws you take with each cigarette. Reduce the number of cigarettes you smoke until two days before your cessation date you are smoking only one-fourth of a cigarette.

- Seek professional assistance if you can't do it on your own

Sometimes making an effort is not sufficient. Without your knowledge, your dependence on cigarettes has grown so severe that you may now require medical intervention to surmount it. If you consume up to 25 cigarettes per day and your first cigarette within 30 minutes of waking up, you are severely dependent on nicotine.

Nicotine-inhibiting medications such as patches, gum, sprays, and inhalers can be used to suppress cravings. Some non-nicotine substitutes may even aid you while you are experiencing nicotine withdrawal. One thing to keep in mind, however, is that you cannot cease smoking based solely on medication. You must also undertake behavior modification to achieve success in this endeavor.

- Prepare in advance for your cessation day

When you eventually approach the D-Day, you must ensure that you are prepared to handle cravings and withdrawal symptoms. When you sense the urge to smoke, consume a portion of fresh fruit or chew sugar-free gum. You can also consume other nutritious substances.

Keep track of your accomplishments so far. It helps you remain motivated and focused on your objective. Reward yourself for your hard work and incredible success thus far with a movie, a lengthy walk, a visit with friends, or any other enjoyable activity.

Get rid of everything associated with smoking, including cigarettes, lighters, ashtrays, match boxes, and ashes, as well as the odor.

- Give up on Quit Day

You will accomplish nothing by flinging your habit into the nearest trash can and yelling, "Here, I quit!" You must actually STOP smoking, and when you do, you will observe immediate physical changes. You can feel an improvement in your blood circulation, blood pressure, and pulse rate as the oxygen levels in your body return to normal.

The greatest aspect of the smoking cessation program is that, within a few days, you observe dramatic, highly motivating changes. When you observe that your efforts are bringing about the desired change, you will remain committed to your objective and eventually achieve it.

# Negative Effects Of Cigarette/Tobacco Emissions

There are approximately 4000 chemical compounds in cigarette smoke, and more than 40 of them are known to cause cancer. The most well-known components of cigarette smoke are nicotine, tar, and carbon monoxide. Nicotine is primarily responsible for cigarette addiction, while tar has a carcinogenic effect and carbon monoxide may contribute to cardiovascular diseases (heart attacks and strokes). According to research conducted in 2018, even light smoking (one to five cigarettes per day) can be problematic (Titan-Crete, 2015). Smoking is blamed for nearly all forms of cancer and respiratory diseases (such as chronic obstructive pulmonary disease), while passive smoking also plays a significant role.

Additionally, the passive smoker is at risk for cardiovascular disease, stroke, lung cancer, respiratory illness, and respiratory complications. The smoker's lungs have purified the smoke that exits their mouth or nostrils. Thus, it is less hazardous than the vapor produced by a cigarette's flame. The last smoke a smoker exhales contains three times more carbon monoxide than the previous smoke. Passive smokers inhale the same amount of carbon monoxide as active smokers after thirty minutes in a room with smoke.

Exposure to cigarette smoke during pregnancy increases the risk of minimal embryonic development, missed abortion, prenatal death, low birth weight, infant malformations, and sudden infant death syndrome. Infants and children who are exposed to passive smoking are at risk for asthma, increased paroxysms, respiratory infections, otitis media, and sudden infant death syndrome. The use of tobacco by parents correlates with an increase in the proportion of adolescents who smoke.

After smoking, surfaces (furniture, doors, draperies, pillows, carpets, walls) are left with remnants of the puff of smoke, as well as dust. Nicotine, 3-ethylpyridine, phenol, cresols, naphthalene, formaldehyde, and special nitrosamines are present in the compounds.

Significant health benefits after one week of quitting smoking include the cessation of immediate reduction of pulmonary function (reduced progression of chronic obstructive lung disease), reduced risk of post-surgical complications, sudden cardiac death, low birth weight, and pregnancy complications. There is a low risk of pulmonary infections, fewer asthma attacks, and enhanced epidermis.

Why there are smokers

Despite all the negative effects of smoking, there are a large number of smokers worldwide because cigarettes provide excellent spiritual clarity. Smoking is an integral aspect of daily life. It helps smokers relax, relieves tension, and improves their cognitive function. Some smokers believe that quitting would cause them to gain weight.

Tobacco is as addictive as narcotics (as an agent that alters mood and behavior). Nicotine is one thousand times more potent than alcohol, ten to one hundred times more potent than barbiturates, and five to ten times more potent than cocaine or morphine. Inhaling one to two cartons of cigarettes per day, the smoker consumes 200 to 400 doses per day for years. This consistent consumption of a drug with a rapid onset of action (which effects mood, concentration, and performance) eventually leads to dependence.

Nicotine diffuses into the brain quicker than any drug administered intravenously, as it diffuses intraarterially through the lungs within seven seconds of the first cigarette inhalation, after the heartbeat has passed through the lungs. In the forebrain, nicotinic receptors 42 activate dopamine. Dopamine is essentially the pleasure hormone, so when a person smokes and nicotine enters the brain, dopamine produces the same effect. The delight of smoking is what causes addiction.

Nicotine addiction is a persistent and chronic condition. It was confirmed that the researchers recruited individuals who had never smoked in their lives and obtained individuals who had not smoked for many years. They gave them each a cigarette to smoke. In the Positron Emission Tomography – Computed Tomography (PET-CT) scan examination (the test that reveals the brain's metabolism), those who had never smoked cigarettes in their lives did not experience anything at all. In contrast, a single cigarette reactivated the entire region of the ex-smoker's brain that corresponds to nicotinic receptors, which had been deactivated after many years of smoking. It is therefore recognized that it prevents relapses. Even a single cigarette can convince a former smoker to begin smoking again. Therefore, when you successfully cease smoking, even if they tell you to smoke one cigarette again, refuse.

Why visit the doctor for smoking cessation?

Approximately 5 to 10 percent of smokers are able to quit smoking promptly without medical assistance. The remaining individuals must obtain medical attention.

The number of nicotine receptors in a person's brain can also affect how many cigarettes he or she will consume. Each cigarette provides varying degrees of satisfaction and addresses the conditions generated by nicotine's allure. Quitting smoking has more to do with physical dependence than with a forceful personality.

Therefore, you should seek medical attention. Quitting smoking is a medical procedure that varies from individual to individual. You may be required to take medication that differs among smokers. Later in this book, I will discuss the various medical strategies that your doctor may recommend for ceasing smoking, based on the factors that influence your smoking behavior. You will require multiple consultations with your physician. In addition to the doctor's advice and prescriptions (pills, etc.), your willingness to cease smoking will play a significant role.

## Benefits Of Quitting

The benefits of ceasing are experienced almost immediately.

Regardless of age, the risk of developing a severe smoking-related disease is drastically reduced following cessation. However, your risk will be significantly reduced if you quit smoking sooner. Research has confirmed that individuals who quit smoking before the age of fifty reduce their risk of premature death to the same level as those who do not smoke. And even if you quit smoking at the age of sixty, your risk of dying at any given age is reduced by approximately 39 percent compared to smokers.

Here are some of the advantages you will receive if you stop smoking:

You reduce your risk of developing cancer, heart disease, peripheral vascular disease, and chronic obstructive pulmonary disease, which are all caused by smoking.

In addition, you reduce the likelihood of developing conditions that, although not life-threatening, can cause you and your life problems. This includes erectile dysfunction, impotence, optic neuropathy, fertility issues, macular degeneration (the breakdown of the macula, a tissue at the back of the eye), cataracts, tooth loss, psoriasis, and Raynaud's phenomenon (where the fingers turn blue or white when exposed to cold).

Additionally, if you are expectant, you decrease the likelihood of experiencing complications.

In the event that you have been a smoker since adolescence or early adulthood:

If you quit smoking before the age of thirty-five, the difference between your life expectancy and that of nonsmokers will be minimal.

If you cease smoking before the age of fifty, you cut your risk of dying from complications caused by smoking-related diseases in half.

Even if you have already been diagnosed with a smoking-related illness, such as heart problems or COPD, it is never too late to cease. As soon as you stop smoking, your prognosis will improve.

The following is a timeline of the health benefits you will receive after quitting smoking.

Seventy-two hours from now: You will have a simpler time breathing. The bronchial tubes will begin to relax, and your vitality level will increase.

One month: Your skin's appearance will improve due to an increase in skin perfusion.

Within three to nine months, respiration, wheezing, and coughing issues will improve. The lungs' functionality will then increase by up to 10%.

In one year, your risk of suffering a heart attack will decrease to half that of a smoker.

In ten years, your risk of developing lung cancer will decrease to half that of a smoker.

In fifteen years, your heart attack risk will return to that of someone who has never smoked.

There are additional advantages to quitting smoking.

The tobacco odor in your hair, clothing, and home will be eliminated.

Additionally, your breath will no longer scent like stale tobacco.

You will have enhanced senses of taste and scent. Drinks and foods will scent and taste significantly better.

You will receive higher insurance premiums.

Your finances will be positively affected. If you previously smoked twenty cigarettes per day, you will save well over $2,000 annually.

You are also more likely to have a positive outlook on life and feel good about yourself and your surroundings.

# Organizing Your Stop Smoking Plan

Smoking is both a physical and mental addiction. Because nicotine in cigarettes provides the brain with a temporary pleasurable feeling, it is highly addictive. Therefore, when you attempt to eliminate your daily nicotine intake, you will likely experience cravings and physical withdrawal. You may have smoked to alleviate depression, anxiety, tension, or even sheer boredom due to the "feel good" sensation that it provides. Simultaneously, you may have used smoking as a daily ritual, something that must be performed daily. You may have become accustomed to smoking while drinking coffee in the morning, taking breaks from school or work, or even while commuting home after a particularly long day. Perhaps you have been influenced by your peers and family, primarily because it is an integral part of your ability to relate to them.

In order to successfully cease smoking, you must address both the addiction and the accompanying habits.

When deciding to quit smoking, it is essential to plan ahead and ensure that you are prepared and entirely committed to doing so. A solid plan that will work for you will not only address the long-term obstacles you may face on the road to recovery, but also the short-term obstacles you may face along the way. To assist you in identifying the therapies and techniques that will be most beneficial to you, carefully consider the following inquiries.

Can you be considered more of a gregarious smoker?

Do you desire cigarettes or tobacco with each and every meal?

Do you experience the urge to smoke when you're feeling down?

How many cigarettes do you smoke daily to soothe yourself? A pack? Or are a few twigs sufficient?

Can you associate your smoking behaviors with other addictions, such as gambling and alcoholism, that you may have?

Are you willing to discuss your condition with a therapist or counselor?

Do you think it's acceptable to undergo acupuncture or hypnotherapy?

Participating in fitness programs intrigues you?

Remember the acronym START when beginning your plan to cease smoking:

Set a date when you'll retire. This date must be within the next two weeks so that you have sufficient time to prepare before losing your willpower. If you smoke at your place of employment, choose the weekend as your cessation date.

Inform your family and acquaintances. It is essential that they are aware of your intention to cease so that they can assist and support you. You may seek out a co-quitter if you so choose.

Anticipate the obstacles you will face while ceasing and plan accordingly. Most individuals who attempt to quit smoking begin smoking again within three months. Therefore, consider what you can do to help you overcome minor obstacles such as withdrawal symptoms or cravings.

Eliminate cigarettes from your existence. Do not even consider abandoning your emergency kit. Everything that will serve as a reminder of your addiction must be eliminated.

Consult your doctor. Before you begin planning, it is imperative that you consult a medical professional so that appropriate medications and alternatives can be suggested.

Side consequences of quitting smoking

During recuperation, you may experience the following common adverse effects:

DESIRES - These may be initial areas of strength, but they typically only last a few seconds. If you oppose everyone, they will gradually become weaker over time.

As your body adjusts to not smoking, anxiety and difficulty concentrating or resting will diminish. Unwinding and deep breathing can be beneficial.

Peevishness, indignation, disquiet, and a despondent disposition are all typical; avoid overreacting. Simply recognize that you will be near to home for a while and that it will pass.

An increase in appetite and weight gain - this could last up to a month. The proper planning can be beneficial.

Additional uncommon adverse effects you may experience, which will also pass, include:

Cold symptoms such as coughing and wheezing

Stoppage/Constipation

Instability or dizziness Mouth ulcers.

Long-term, you will observe that these adverse effects become more susceptible, and you will consider smoking less. If you experience severe or persistent adverse effects, it may be beneficial to consult a medical professional.

How to maintain motivation when quitting smoking

To ensure that you retain your smoking cessation inspiration and quit smoking inspiration, it is always best to keep things uncomplicated. You suddenly become fatigued by smoking. Either the fear of it, its cost, its effect on your family and your health, or the control and enslavement of compulsion. Instead of using one of these - or even all of these - as your motivation, choose to quit smoking because you'll enjoy your life so much more as a non-smoker, and because you'll enjoy the freedom from so many negative perspectives, and - most importantly - because you'll enjoy the positive things that opportunity brings to your life.

Schedules designed to assist you in overcoming tobacco/cigarette addictions

Perhaps the greatest obstacle many people confront at the start of quitting is their ingrained desires. Some cravings are due to your body's genuine need for nicotine, while others are related to your daily routines.

Changing your regimen can assist you in avoiding the triggers that signal to your brain that it's time for a cigarette.

Here are some ideas for exercises you can do instead of smoking when you would ordinarily reach for a cigarette:

At the start of dawn, take a shower with coffee or tea, then switch to a different beverage, cup, or location to consume it.

At morning tea, sit in a better location or with different people, read a magazine, or peruse your online entertainment.

Change the appearance of your home computer by relocating your workspace or redesigning.

After a dinner - enjoy a walk

After work, exercise or reflect

Prior to dinner - make your dinner schedule prior to dinner

With alcoholic beverages, switch to a different drink or hold your drink in your smoking hand.

As you plan your next endeavor, inhale deeply.

As a reward, listen to music or receive a piece of natural product.

When you are around a smoker, chew gum or carry a bottle of water.

Before watching television, rearrange the furniture, squeeze a stress ball, and perform simple stretches.

Before slumber, enjoy a warm beverage or read a book.

Remember that every time you resist a craving and do something else instead, it is a victory in your quest to quit: you are assisting your brain in severing the connection between the action and the cigarette.

The more options you have to divert your attention,

the more desirable. The following are a few additional ideas that you can try whenever:

Gradually savor a glass of water. Have fun with a companion. Call a confidante. ▫ Play a game on your mobile device. Ask your partner or a companion for a shoulder rub. Attempt some sowing. ▫ Apply some hand balm. Perform a jigsaw or crossword puzzle. Peel an orange. Consider the reasons for your decision and visualize a positive future.

Medical benefits of quitting smoking

Quitting smoking is one of the most important steps individuals can take to improve their health. This is true regardless of their age or length of smoking history.

Stopping smoking:

Enhances wellbeing status and improves personal fulfillment.

Reduces the risk of sudden death and can add up to ten years to the future.

Reduces the risk of certain adverse health effects, including poor conceptional health, cardiovascular diseases, chronic obstructive pulmonary disease (COPD), and malignant growth.

Beneficial for individuals previously diagnosed with coronary disease or COPD.

Improves the vitality of expectant women and their offspring and infants.

Reduces the financial burden that smoking places on smokers, health care systems, and society.

While quitting earlier in life yields greater health benefits, quitting at any point in life is beneficial to your health. In fact, even those who have smoked for an extended period of time or who have smoked heavily will benefit from ceasing.

Quitting smoking is the most effective method to protect loved ones, coworkers, and friends from the health risks associated with secondhand smoke exposure.

## Conclusion

Cessation of smoking can improve your appearance. As blood circulation improves, the epidermis absorbs more oxygen and nutrients. This can help you cultivate a superior coloring. If you remain tobacco-free, the stains on your fingertips and toenails will disappear. You may attempt to observe your teeth becoming whiter.

In addition to the health benefits, one of the benefits of quitting cigarettes is the money you will save. There are online calculators that determine how much more lavish you will become.

Reward yourself by spending some of the money on something enjoyable.

## How To Stop Using - The Rapid Method

However, following this method is difficult, and the risk of relapse is substantial. Nonetheless, there are methods to prepare for the big cut. In this way, you prepare your mind for the upcoming major change in your life, mitigating the effects of the abrupt halt.

SET A DATE

The first step is to establish a date. Typically, individuals quit smoking on a specific date, such as their birthday, New Year's, or Christmas. However, you can resign on a specific day, such as Monday. And resolve to cease smoking every Monday so that you have multiple opportunities to do so.

MAKE CHANGES BEFORE THE DAY YOU QUIT

This is intended to "trick" your psyche and aid you in the process of quitting. Change the brand of cigarettes you smoke, for instance, if you made the decision to cease smoking on December

25 and want to quit on January 30. Select one you've never experienced before. The reason for this is because the change in chemistry affects the flavor of the cigarette and alters the experience. It is unlikely to produce the "ahhhh" effect.

The effectiveness of this method has been demonstrated by the fact that it "confuses" the dopamine flow. Your brain will anticipate fulfillment, only to be let down. It will "de-automatize" smoking for you and strengthen your resolve to cease.

LIVE THROUGH THE FIRST WEEK

When the time comes to cease smoking, be sure to stop completely; for example, as soon as you wake up in the morning, dispose of your cigarettes, ashtray, and lighters. You should not have anything in your home that will remind you of smoking.

Plan what you will do when you experience the urge to smoke. You can substitute drinking for smoking. You can brush your teeth or perform twenty push-ups to take your mind off smoking.

Additionally, you can wear one of those motivational wristbands to remind you of your decision to cease smoking. It should be large and clearly marked so that everyone can read it. The wristband serves two purposes: (1) to serve as a reminder of your mission to quit smoking, and (2) to be worn when you feel tempted to give up. Velcro it to your forearm! The discomfort of the crack will eliminate the desire to smoke!

Reward yourself after you've survived the first week. Commemorate your first week without cigarettes by purchasing something you enjoy; however, nothing ostentatious. Start with a small reward.

ENDURE A FULL MONTH

Some individuals have found it helpful to trick their imaginations into believing they will only abstain for one month.

This increases their motivation because, in the back of their minds, they anticipate returning to the habit at the conclusion of the first month.

However, after one month, evaluate your desire to smoke. Ask yourself, "Do I truly want to waste all my hard work?" Then, attempt to deceive yourself for another month. This makes quitting, even if done abruptly, much simpler to endure.

Give up for the sake of your loved ones

In all honesty, no one enjoys watching a loved one smoke their life away. Your family is unhappy with your smoking, and they will be ecstatic if you cease. Most smokers avoid smoking in the presence of their loved ones; this demonstrates that they have sufficient regard for their loved ones. Now, if you want your affection for your loved ones to be complete, quitting smoking would be the ideal gift to give them.

John, a former smoker, answered that he quit for his family when asked why he quit. John began smoking during his senior year of high school. Throughout his early adulthood and adulthood, he smoked. On the day before the birthday of his youngest son, he developed severe chest pains and was confined to the hospital.

John received the greatest shock of his life when he awoke in a hospital bed and learned that he had suffered a heart attack and required two stents. At that moment, John began to experience a glimpse of his future; he abruptly felt 90 at the age of 64. When he saw his anxious wife and children on the other side of the bed, he knew it was time to resign. John explained that he did not want to lose out on his sons starting their own families as one of the most compelling reasons for his decision.

Similar to John, Mary in the earlier story had to halt when her granddaughter looked her in the eyes and said, "Grandma, you stink!" This was sufficient to convince Mary to resign. Even if you don't want to resign for any other reason, you should quit for the sake of your loved ones if you have a wonderful family.

4. give up for financial reasons

Another compelling reason to cease smoking is the hole it creates in your wallet. If you settle down and calculate how much you spend on cigarettes every day, you will realize that you have been spending an excessive amount of money on a habit that is quite harmful.

Robert, a former smoker who ceased for financial reasons, stated in an interview that, as a businessman, he had calculated how much money he would save daily if he did not smoke. The realization that he could save up to $84 per week by quitting smoking opened his eyes to the numerous things he could do if he decided to do so. He discovered that if he stopped smoking for one week and one month, he could purchase an e-reader and the most recent smartphone, respectively.

His new discovery prompted him to take proactive measures to quit smoking. On occasion, when he experienced withdrawal symptoms, he would use a portion of the money he had saved to purchase himself some threats. Robert and his wife were able to pay off their mortgage after approximately six years because he quit smoking and put his life in order.

Which or how many of the aforementioned causes would prompt you to leave your job? Think carefully. Once you have responded, proceed to the next section where we will discuss how to resign.

Third Section: How to Quit

As previously stated, smoking is a hazardous habit, and in order to quit, you must have a plan of action. People usually believe they can cease smoking on their own, which is why they fail. If you must quit a bad habit, such as smoking, you must replace it with a healthy alternative; otherwise, you will relapse.

Therefore, here are three things you must do in order to stop smoking:

1. Reflect 2. Prepare

3. Quit

1. Think ◆◆◆

The reasoning aspect relates to the motivation for quitting. If you do not have a compelling reason for quitting, you may relapse within days. Consider the question, "Why do I want to do this?" Do you wish to do it for the sake of your health? For your household? Regarding your finances? Because you are sick and weary of the unhealthy habit, yes. Ensure that your reason is sufficiently persuasive.

Now, if you have determined a reason to resign, you should record it in a journal. This journal will be utilized to monitor your progress (more on this in a later section of this chapter).

2. Prepare ◆◆◆

The second stage is to prepare for the upcoming task. Here, you are required to develop healthy behaviors to replace your unhealthy smoking habit. Next, select an end date and keep it in mind. Record your departure date in the journal you received earlier.

Additionally, you must prepare for withdrawal symptoms. A number of disagreeable withdrawal symptoms accompany quitting smoking, including:

• Restlessness: when attempting to cease, many smokers experience feelings of restlessness or excess energy. This is because your body is attempting to recover, which is causing the sensation of restlessness. You may also experience difficulty resting. If you feel excessively energized while attempting to stop smoking, you could channel that energy into exercise.

• Feeling tense, irritable, and unable to concentrate: this is another withdrawal symptom you are likely to encounter when you cease smoking. Typically, these sensations will make you feel somewhat at ease; all you need to do is relax, as they will pass. Don't be too critical of yourself

• Feeling apprehensive and nervous: quitting smoking may increase your anxiety level. If you believe you cannot handle your emotions on your own, you should assemble a support group. Your team may consist of family members, a healthcare provider, and a counselor. Conversation with your support group will help you forget about nicotine. So, whenever you experience a craving, contact your support group.

As part of your preparation, you must acquire some instruments for quitting. Medications, such as nicotine replacement therapy (NRT) and combination therapy, are included. You must consult with your healthcare provider for direction on how to proceed.

You also need a strong support network, which could include friends, family, coworkers, or anyone else you believe could be instrumental in helping you overcome your destructive habit.

Prepare your exit plan ◆◆◆

Your cessation plan should include the date you intend to stop smoking. Other elements that should be included in your quit plan are: • the reason you are resigning. Create a list of the various factors for quitting. (Your justification should be convincing enough)

• Determine from whom you will receive support (could be your wife, spouse, siblings, friends, or other members of your family); • Identify your trigger situations;

• How you will reward yourself for reaching important milestones

• Tools to assist in quitting • Techniques for managing impulses

You must organize and document your quit plan, preferably using a journal to monitor your progress. After completing that, you are ultimately prepared to quit.

3. Quit ◆◆◆

Now that the D-day has arrived, here are the tasks you must complete on the first day:

• Collect all cigarettes in your residence and dispose of them. Be sure to thoroughly search your home and all hiding places for cigarettes (glove compartments, sweater pockets, etc.).

• Eliminate all objects affiliated with cigarettes and smoking. For instance, dispose of your matches, lighters, ashtrays, cigarette cases, etc. Not only should these items be eliminated, but they should also be replaced with alternatives such as nutritious snacks and gum.

• Evaluate your reasons for quitting. Have you discovered additional reasons to give up? Add them to your existing list.

• Ensure that your prescribed withdrawal medications are readily available.

• Exercising frequently will prevent you from thinking about smoke. Additionally, consume an abundance of healthy items.

• Get a decent night's sleep

• Above all else, eliminate limiting beliefs; if you believe you can succeed, you will. Also, eliminate all negative notions, as they can undermine your confidence. Positive thinking will assist you tremendously.

## BATHING IN ICE

The next irrational thought that entered my mind was the desire to boost my immunity by immersing in ice. I showered in ice throughout the entire winter, even in 35-degree frost. I could not withstand more than one minute of barefoot walking in the snow around the home.

The conclusion of all time!

This is what I will tell you about ice soaking. I lost a great deal of time but gained a wealth of valuable experience.

You shouldn't immerse in ice without prior preparation, and certainly not while intoxicated.

Only during bathing procedures with a birch broom should one begin bathing in ice with icy water. What a marvelous innovation, the Russian bath! The ice was melted on birch timber and saturated with field daisies and wormwood. It should be producing as much steam as chest fire and heel sparkles. Then, in your first-born suit, you rush out onto the lawn with a bucket of icy water and immerse yourself in ice. Unfiltered from the container. Apply liquid to the thorax and back. In any case, do not pour it on your head; do not heed to fools who say otherwise. The wooden mackintosh will be your last garment if your central microprocessor (brain) fails.

After scooping up a fistful of water, you simply rinsing your face and rubbing it behind your ears. Do not touch the parietal and occipital regions of the cranium. You are like awakening up... The connection between slumber and reality has frayed. You will experience an unprecedented surge of vitality, indescribable relief, and joy. You appreciate the present, the universe, and yourself.

You are confronted by the universe. Butt-naked. Within the snow-covered lawn's center. Want to commune with God? Raise your cranium and take in the night sky. You must still discover the secrets of this universe, but not today.

And now, before you could acquire a cold on your family heirlooms, dash back to your hot bath. Pour boiling water over the stones, and, as the burning vapor hisses, ascend to the top shelf. And now, the most intriguing portion. Instantaneously, the body's temperature rises to 39 degrees. This is exactly what we desired.

Viruses can be eradicated by bathing in cold. Including those that are not yet manifested by a specific disease, but already sap our body's vitality.

One icy bath is sufficient. Do not neglect to draft a will in advance if you intend to repeat the bathing procedure multiple times. It will be necessary for those who continue to love you. Avoid being egotistical. Everything should be approached with moderation. Gradually, the arrangement evolved.

So, if you heed my advice, you may reach the central portion of my book.

I will continue recounting my exploits.

## STARVATION

I became intrigued in therapeutic starvation a year later. At the time, I was sensitive to odors. Even recalling these days causes my intestines to contract. I feel apprehensive. I've experimented with various forms of treatment in an effort to comply with all applicable laws and proven technologies. And occurrences like this are common.

Imagine that there are laws. Do you believe the cranium is the most important part of our body? You are in error. Ass. Because a cranium cannot exist without an ass, otherwise the body will become intoxicated and Beyonce will be played at your funeral. However, the truth is that you will not listen.

I starved for the first two months according to the following schedule: one day of hunger followed by one day of eating, two days of hunger followed by one day of eating, and three days of hunger followed by one day of eating. In addition, in a circle... An infinite circle ... It was fascinating to experience this for myself - am I a trembling beast or do I have the truth? How strong my testicles are and in similar situations.

People on the Internet claim that on the third day, the consciousness shifts and it becomes uncomplicated and easy. No way! After three days, I was ready to chew the wall. But I had to persevere. It was a valuable lesson. Lesson in self-awareness, willpower training, and the accumulation of personal vitality.

My relatives were concerned about me and attempted to strike me in the head by any means necessary. And my exam was twice as difficult. I desired to grasp my level of coolness and the limits of impossibility. Maximum time I could survive without food is one week. However, there are men who can survive forty days without sustenance; this is abnormal. "I ate" only water and nothing else.

Once, I found myself thinking that this is merely a game and that panic, not hunger, kills people. When discussing this with my new fiancée, a well-educated attorney, I learned that she believes cannibalism in cases of survival is justified. This is where I disagree. I would never want to be stranded with her on a barren island. It is preferable to perish as a human rather than a beast.

After that... I subsequently ceased this practice. I acquired something and lost something.

Concurrently with my hunger, I ceased drinking beer and switched to a superior product. Two or three glasses of cognac per week are harmless. Stop imbibing beer. This filth murders you at the genetic level from the inside out. Believe me, something is amiss with this beer. Something is not right! There is something added to it.

SPORT

As a result of cybernetics, despite exercising for half of my life, I was unable to lose weight. In the spring, prior to the beach season, the desire to lose weight arrived precisely on schedule. This time, however, I determined, Enough is enough! I am either powerful or weak!

Obviously, I was like a reed when I was starving, but by the end of practice, "extra pounds brought prisoners." It was imperative to take action.

Under the assault of will, which, like nuclear fusion, accumulates over the years... in the secret block of your consciousness, even the most formidable obstacles fall. At the appropriate moment, you draw energy from there to propel your goals, ideas, and initiatives. This is how genuine magic operates. What are your thoughts?

There are three distinct classes of mage. The first are common puppets of malevolent essences; without realizing it, they fulfill another's will for the carrot, and occasionally for the kick. They have no will, but they believe they are gods and urinate to the left and right. The second is characterized as "shit in the ice hole." They appear to be excellent, but there is no motivation.

Third, as you already know, are solitary individuals who are cordial with anyone, and whose power engineering cannot be broken with a crowbar. And they are the ones assisted by entities - ELEMENTAL SPIRITS. These deities do not care how many elderly women you assisted across the street. They do not assist on the basis of "good versus evil." These concepts are foreign to them. They recognize only the POWER, sense it, and allow it to flow through them. So this is how it operates.

A young man approached Shakespeare, who was already well-known as an author at the time, according to historical accounts. He enthusiastically praised the Master's abilities and then exclaimed, "I venerate you so much that I want to be just like you! What can I do to become the next William Shakespeare? William replied with composure, "At the time, I desired to become God, but instead became Shakespeare." Who will you become if you wish to attain godlike status?

The priests of Shao-Lin engage in an intriguing activity. Take a half-squat pose. With feet shoulder-width apart and arms extended. Turn on the timer (coolness dependent, ha ha) and proceed. I repeated this exercise five times and set the timer for thirty minutes. After ten minutes, the extremities become numb and wet. At the twenty-minute mark, hallucinations commence. I recall vividly seeing the multi-armed goddess Shiva dancing on the left with peripheral vision. I disliked her destructive engineering capabilities.

The universe examines you for ugliness by placing a fly on your nose, calling your mobile phone, or having a cat rub against your leg. But you do not budge, you can not. You strike a posture.

There is a golden rule in magic: if it is violated, one can expect trouble from the universe. Take the energy and place it in a hidden compartment. There will come a time when you will require it.

To enhance my power engineering skills, I engage in sports. I had to construct crunches, squats, and dips from two steel pipes. Daily for thirty minutes. Possibly, based on the circumstances. Illnesses such as the common cold and migraines do not qualify. Celebrations are not an acceptable reason either.

The earlier you plan a day, the more it mobilizes you and causes the universe to revolve around you rather than the other way around. And there is no metaphor here. After a year of consistent training "at the limit of opportunities," the flavor of this world will be "at the tip of your tongue." Feel how existence, in paving your path, scatters bread crumbs.

Nobody has destroyed you. Now you are not only physically stronger, but your spirit has become as flexible and resilient as a steel cable. You are capable of holding this world, and more significantly, you could care less about what others say about you.

Simply accept it and do that. You must follow the program to the letter.

As stated in the opening paragraphs, self-pity is the most repulsive trait in a man. Given that I do not know the woman's background, it is difficult for me to offer advice... A woman or child is predominantly feminine. Even in the language of deaf-mutes, it is impossible to convey how they are woven. The complexities of unseen strands penetrate the words and gestures. And perhaps femininity is a magical powder-coated shell with an enigmatic aura.

Some women possess an abundance of femininity.

They will enter the room wearing a collectivefarm sweatshirt and knee-high crocheted boots, but their true nature will not be concealed. Femininity...

Others cannot even afford a costly manicure. Roughness and rudeness emblazoned on their foreheads accompany them everywhere they go... I awoke at 6 a.m. and went to exercise. Then I went to work; in the past, I was an expert at curb tile installation. Hard? The human race adapts to everything.

In this practice of energy storage, it is essential to perform exercises that are challenging to perform. Every time I am performing pull-ups, I must injure myself. Do not lose sight of performance quality at the same time. This is the primary point. I became significantly tougher and more exacting of myself and others.

Exercise:

Slowly count to 25, lingering for a few seconds between each number; then, slowly count backward from 25. Try this while closing your eyes. As you count up, you can imagine being lifted into the heavens, and as you count down, you can imagine descending back to earth.

Today's universe is all about speed. Everyone appears to be in a hurry, yet the majority of people are unhappy and have no idea where they're heading. The pursuit of the next best item is fruitless. Rare is the individual who, regardless of the nature of the present instant, slows down to appreciate it. People are compelled to take anxiety and rush toward a reward and conclusion because there appear to be so many problems and the majority of jobs are focused on resolving them. That is certainly not pleasure. Happiness exists only in the present moment, not in a hypothetical future filled with rewards and successes. Rushing is an additional method of heading nowhere.

How often have you used cigarettes to propel you forward and accomplish tasks, or to unwind and reenergize you? This is detrimental to your mental and physical health: concentration suffers, tension levels rise, and present-moment awareness is impossible. Smoking is not a healthful means of increasing productivity or recharging.

It is imperative to calm down. There is only one life to live, so don't race through it and don't rely on anything that encourages you to hurry. Be still and sluggish.

*Ten minutes of silence and deliberate respiration. Repetition of the mantra "Slow down" Do not hurry. "Appreciate the present moment"

(Share this experience with the hashtag #30DaysCount)

Day 6

Exercise:

Write down on a piece of paper all the labels and adjectives that you and others use to describe you.

For instance, do you consider yourself a son, a daughter, a mother, a father, a student, a teacher, a cashier, a friend, an engineer, an accountant, an employee, an employer, a roommate, a spouse, or a wife? And what adjectives do you use to describe yourself? For instance, do you designate yourself as addicted, unsuccessful, successful, happy, depressed, good, moral, unethical, lustful, greedy, valuable, or worthless? Write down not only the labels and descriptions you perceive, but also what you believe others label you as: do you believe that others see you as a valuable friend, a foolish and incompetent employee, a smoking addict, a highly intelligent and talented worker, etc.? Utilize as much time as necessary to complete a sheet of paper with these labels and descriptions.

After that, rip the paper into multiple fragments and dispose of them. These designations and adjectives have no significance. Not the same as you. Titles cannot define, label, characterize, or control an individual. The majority of individuals corrupt their conscience with such a vocabulary. They are willing to fight, stress out, become unwell, and even die to make these words a reality. Smoking teaches you to identify with specific words, which are merely thoughts. Undevelop them. Thus, you are neither an addict nor a toxic individual. Without the desire or need to poison yourself with cigarettes, you are simply yourself. You need not smoke to designate yourself.

*Ten minutes of silence and deliberate respiration. Repetition of the mantra: "I am not a label, a title, or a description."

(Share your experience with the hashtag #30DaysIdentity)

Day 7

Exercise:

Find a hard object that fits in the palm of your hand, such as a rock, a ball, or a container. Grab this object with both hands and squeeze it as firmly as you can. Squeeze it firmly until you can no longer hold onto it. When finished, discard the item.

If you could continue to squeeze that object indefinitely, you probably would; however, your muscles and nerves have a limit. At some point, you release your grip on the object swiftly and easily. There is no process for the decline; it simply occurs when your body decides it has had enough. The release occurs naturally and effortlessly.

So simple is it to abandon a toxic dependence, habit, thought pattern, addiction, emotion, or behavior. Learn from your body's experience that letting go can be as natural and guilt-free as letting go of the object you were gripping so closely in this exercise. When the time comes to let go, let go.

The time to quit smoking is always...right now. You have the knowledge and awareness to recognize that your body and mind have no beneficial use for cigarettes, despite their prevalence in our culture. Just because those around you are unable to let go of a pernicious dependence does not obligate you to do so as well. There is no legitimate, beneficial, or advantageous purpose to smoke.

*Ten minutes of silence and deliberate respiration. Repeat the mantra: "It is natural to let go. I am able to let go right now."

(Share this experience with the hashtag #30DaysGrip)

Why quitting smoking is most effective

Quitting smoking could have a significant impact on your health and lifestyle. It is never too late to quit smoking to enhance your health significantly. For instance, if you cease smoking in middle age, prior to developing cancer or another severe disease, you avoid the majority of smoking-related future death risks. There is assistance available for those who find it difficult to cease smoking.

What health benefits are associated with quitting smoking?

The advantages commence immediately. At any age, you reduce your likelihood of developing a serious illness. Fortunately, the sooner you quit, the greater the risk reduction. Analysts have discovered that if you cease smoking before the age of 50, your mortality risk is almost identical to that of a nonsmoker. Even if you quit smoking after age 60, your risk of dying at any subsequent age is approximately 39% less than that of a smoker.

If you quit smoking, your risk of succumbing from smoking-related diseases such as heart disease, cancer, chronic obstructive pulmonary disease

(COPD), and peripheral general disease will decrease.

Reduce the risk of acquiring a number of other conditions that, while not life-threatening or life-threating, can cause undesirable complications...

For instance:

Impotence (erection problems)

Fertility difficulties

Optic neuropathy is a disorder that affects the nerve that supplies the eye.

Cataracts

Macular degeneration is a deterioration of tissue in the retina.

Psoriasis

Gum disease

Tooth decay

Osteoporosis in addition to Raynaud's phenomenon (white or blue fingers when subjected to cold).

Pregnancy concerns


If you have smoked since you were an adolescent or young adult:


If you quit smoking before approximately the age of 35, your life expectancy is only slightly lower than that of individuals who have never smoked.

If you cease smoking before the age of 50, you reduce your risk of dying from smoking-related diseases by fifty percent.

Never is it too late to stop smoking for health benefits. Even if you presently have COPD or cardiovascular disease, quitting smoking will significantly improve your prognosis.

Four additional benefits of quitting smoking:

No longer will your breath scent of stale tobacco. Additionally, the smell of stale tobacco will be eliminated from your clothing, hair, and residence.

Foods and beverages scent and taste significantly better.

You will receive significantly improved premium quotes for health, medical, and life insurance.

You're likely to feel fantastic about yourself!!

## How To Stop Smoking

If you desire to successfully quit smoking, you must first conduct an honest self-examination and then identify and implement techniques and strategies that match your personality and aid you in dangerous situations. Let's examine some exclusive recommendations that will assist you in quitting smoking:

Create a list of the reasons you wish to quit.

People who desire to bring about change can be successful if they write down their objectives. Therefore, write down all the reasons you want to quit smoking, such as the money you will save and the increased athletic stamina. Keep this list in a location where you will always see it. Include new reasons as they come to mind.

Create a list of everything you enjoy about smoke.

Take a sheet of paper and draw a line down its middle. Now, on one side, list the things you like about smoking, and on the other side, list the things you detest about smoking, such as how it can affect your health, family, and work. Examine the inventory over time and make adjustments. If you have the courage, attempt to get feedback from family and friends about aspects of your tobacco use that they dislike. When the number of negative aspects exceeds the number of positive aspects, you are ready to give up.

Establish a deadline to quit smoking

Establishing a deadline will provide you with a target to strive for. Choose a date that is two to three weeks after the day you establish the time limit. The short deadline will encourage you to remain on track and not find an excuse to quit smoking. People look for reasons to resume smoking again, after all. Do not be one of these individuals.

Do not squander time.

We frequently resolve to quit smoking, but we cannot do so because of a timed fact. When someone suggests we cease, we excuse them by saying we'll give it a try tomorrow. The following day, we make the same excuse and say the same thing. As time progresses, it becomes increasingly difficult for us to quit smoking. To quit smoking, we must avoid this and begin the process immediately.

Inform your family, acquaintances, and coworkers that you intend to quit smoking.

Friends and family always provide support and assistance. Smoking by family members makes quitting more difficult. If possible, attempt to persuade other family members or acquaintances who smoke to quit at the same time. A collaborative endeavor can be easier than working alone.

## Restating Mental Sobriety

Your mind has always been stronger than nicotine, but the moment you willingly opened the door to illegal substances, you damaged the part of your mind that knows you should always view the act of smoking cigarettes as inherently harmful to your body – as something that will cause you harm.

Obviously, we cannot see our mind because it is a portion of energy; therefore, only the spirit within us can perceive and comprehend it. Intelligent mind control requires total sobriety to be effective. The only way to maintain an intelligent demeanor is through coherent thought, which enables you to evaluate your behavior in any given circumstance as good, poor, wise, or foolish.

The rejection of items that you consciously know are harmful to your life should be automatic. You may reach a point where you believe that everyone dies eventually, so why not accept it and continue smoking? However, you must recognize that this is suicidal; in this instance, your mind is not your ally, but your adversary. The words "Yes" and "No" are both filled with potent energy.

If you're sincere about quitting, you should decide to achieve the highest level of sobriety; this is the point at which you can reason and dismiss any selfish or negative thoughts. Then it will be simpler and more natural for you to always have absolute control over your conduct.

The Strength of Words

Words are extremely potent. You've been using them your entire life, but to be successful in this endeavor, you must increase your awareness of their actual value and potency. This comprehension can help you move mountains!

You must think words for them to have a powerful effect on your mind and existence. Concentrating on a word or concept for an extended period of time is called focussing. You will then recognize the power of words, which will not only assist you in putting an end to your negative behaviors but also in maintaining your positive ones. Because the secret relies on word association, you are able to maintain your self-proposed goals. Walk in the significance of every word you ponder and every word you utter.

For example, suppose you wish to quit smoking. Your body and mind may be physically dependent on nicotine, but your spirit has never been and never will be. Your spirit utilizes the power of words. The fact that you are thinking "I want to quit smoking" and have taken the steps to purchase this book is evidence that you are now thinking the correct thoughts.

You must now give them more autonomy than the phrase, "I need a cigarette." Then you will indeed achieve victory!

How do you do this? I recommend spending time alone with yourself and your thoughts to concentrate on the words you wish to invest with more vitality and force. Perform this concentration as frequently as possible each day.

Contrary to prevalent belief, you do not need to be behind closed doors in order to meditate or concentrate on any idea at any given time. No one else occupies your mental territory. It makes no difference if you are in the largest of throngs. You may be surrounded by chronic, hacking smokers who relish their assault on their bodies.

You will not be disturbed because you are cultivating a distinct interpretation and perception of the reality of cigarette smoking.

As you observe your mind and the words it's using to persuade you to light up a cigarette, you want to capture and eliminate that string of words, and then replace it with the exact opposite, which should be the reason why it's so imprudent to light up that cigarette.

For instance, suppose you're having a difficult day and pondering, "I really need a cigarette. Another will not destroy me."

In your mind, this is a defective and destructive alien. You want to get quiet and challenge that thought and sensation with the opposite: "I really don't need a cigarette. One more would be fatal." And you repeat this until you are convinced by the logic.

It will not always be difficult because you want to resign.

By performing this exercise, you are invoking the power of your mind, seizing control of your mind, and enabling it to produce the beneficial hormones that will cause these cravings to subside and become less frequent. This is how one cultivates a levelheaded mind. And you are not required to tell anyone what you are doing!

From your new perspective, it is simple to see how accepting a cigarette from a friend is analogous to ingesting poison. You become sufficiently sober to realize that you are in peril and that your friend is acting ignorantly, whether intentionally or not.

When we are ill, we require medical attention. However, smoking is not an organic disease, so you must take a different approach to quit. It is impossible to lose with word-energy; it is a safe and effective method to stimulate the mind.

Doctors, therapists, and self-help experts will tell you that you need this medication or that therapy to cure your addiction, but in reality, all you need is your own mental strength.

Nicotine withdrawal, you may say? Everything falls under the same category. The body is subservient to the intellect. Simply begin the practice of redirecting your focus to other, more productive pursuits and interests.

You are now beginning to teach yourself what words are and what they mean, whether through introspection or conversation with others. Go into session, instruct yourself on the sage knowledge you've acquired, and accomplish resolution by putting energy to work and leveraging your own self-confidence.

You can only exercise mind control in sobriety if you can think logically, so hold back and conduct yourself in accordance with the fundamental essence of logic. This argument demonstrates how power actually functions to guarantee a change in you – at no cost.

Why would you want it any other way besides under your mind's control? And remember, you will never have to communicate with others. Aha! Reacquisition of power! Check and finish.

This is the moment with which you should connect. It concerns the control your intellect has over your body.

You did not associate with this as a smoker because your spirit was constantly on the move. Perhaps you consumed too much alcohol, lived the nightlife for too long while smoking like a chimney, and cursed in every conceivable way for no apparent reason. Your mind has lost equilibrium, concentration, a decent vocabulary, and logic.

You have become uncritical and insensitive, which has allowed your mind to feed on an increasing amount of negativity, clouding your judgment, sense of caution, and concern for matters affecting you and your health. You will ultimately lose if you are not considerate in these ways, and this is all the more reason for you to have a thorough understanding of issues that are vital to you.

If you had mental control, you would have never started smoking, because your common sense would have dissuaded you from engaging in something so imprudent, given the vast number of negative side effects associated with smoking.

If you find what I say offensive, then your mind is reinforcing your smoking habit rather than attempting to end it. I am instructing you on how to think and retrain your mind; in order to rid yourself of the addiction, you must now despise the way you used to think and act, or you will remain feeble and submissive to nicotine.

REASON and LOGIC say smoking is UNNATURAL and FOOLISH.


Restoring the smoker's mental health

Smoking is notorious for desensitizing its users. Typically, you have little esteem or regard for nonsmokers. The majority of smokers suffer from this, according to statistical evidence. And frequently, smokers are insensitive not on purpose, but as a result of a mental fracture.

Once you begin to implement the word consciousness I discussed, your mind will be better able to comprehend how those in your life who do not smoke have been affected, whether at work or at home. Those individuals, as well as your body, will be ecstatic about your endeavor to quit smoking and recover.

People who have successfully ceased smoking almost always tell me how EMANCLING it is to be free of cigarettes.

You will also value the ability to overcome smoker's bias. Frequently, the mind of a smoker has an irrational aversion to quitting smoking. It is easy to rationalize smoking with phrases such as "I could be hit by a bus tomorrow" or "We all have to die of something" or "It's my guilty pleasure" or "I only smoke outside" or "Nonsmokers die of lung cancer all the time!" etc.

But as your mind clears, you begin to wonder, 'What have I really gained from smoking for the past (insert number of years)?"

Your intellect may immediately say, "Enjoy!" Because it may be that you enjoy smoking after a meal, after intercourse, just before bed, as soon as you wake up, or perhaps as a comforting habit throughout the day. Because it became an extremely valuable habit.

However, what was the true value of this delectable habit? Consistently focusing on positive word energy should make the answer crystal obvious.

Your mind created a potent illusion because it was of no greater value to you than a hole in the cranium.

A Personal and Powerful Success Story: Lorenzo Walden!

Meet my honorable acquaintance, Lorenzo Walden. We used to attend church together several decades ago. When we met, we were both Christians. I will tell you about his smoking history.

From 1981 to 1982, I worked in the Lauderhill, Florida, location of the Lindsey Lumber supply store, where Lorenzo and his family shopped. One of the two women who entered the store before I met him was his wife. Two to three weeks later, Lorenzo entered the store after having a very cordial conversation with us.

It wasn't long, however, before Mr. Lorenzo and I began discussing our (then) shared faith. It was a pleasant and harmonious conversation, and we immediately connected. During our conversation, my new friend Lorenzo was so elated that he did a few hops and elegant strides up and down the store aisle.

Consequently, Christian energy was high between us, and I could perceive his sincerity. We were on the same page, and I felt at ease speaking with him about reasonable matters.

Okay, well, Lorenzo quickly disclosed that he was a smoker, and where I'm from in Jamaica, smoking is strictly forbidden because it is believed to be a transgression against the Lord. I immediately moved to charge the spirit brother with biblical smoking. I made my potent point in a stealthy and courteous manner, which was quite simple given how well we had connected.

First, I asked an inquisitive question: "So, you smoke?" I said to him.

Lorenzo responded, "Yes." My community allows for it."

Now, if you are genuinely prepared, you will enjoy the following section because the power of word-energy is fully demonstrated, and you can imitate the action and reaction based on the command, analysis, and conclusion of your own mind.

I asked Lorenzo, "Are you familiar with the biblical passage that states, "Whom the Son has set free is truly free?"

"Yes, I do," Lorenzo replied.

Then I asked him, "Do you believe 'smoking' constitutes freedom, or is it a condition of servitude?"

After a moment of consideration, Lorenzo stated, "I believe it is bondage."

I responded with "Yes...I concur."

Therefore, Lorenzo saw and acknowledged the reasoning, comprehended the logic I employed, and knew that day would signal the end of his fifteen-year smoking habit! Immediately, in that instant, he decided to STOP SMOKING.

He told me that shortly after the encounter, he almost accepted a cigarette, but as he reached out to take it, his memory kicked in and he discovered a powerful energy, which was secreted from his mind's restored sobriety, and it was enough for him to refuse it.

This event occurred more than three decades ago, and as I sit here writing this, I am proud to say that Lorenzo and I are still closest friends (although he is no longer a Christian) and that he has not smoked a cigarette since then!

And as I sit here penning this, I am aware that the same can be said of you.

I'd like to discuss what it takes to kick the smoking habit for all the reasons I just enumerated, plus many more.

One of the difficulties we face when attempting to cease smoking is a feeling of emptiness. We feel as though there is a void in our existence. The more frequently you smoke, the greater the number of triggers that activate your desire to smoke, making it more difficult to cease.

Our minds are not very good at letting go of habits, but we are excellent at forming new ones. As I will explain throughout this book, rather than simply attempting to cease smoking, we will replace your bad habits with good ones. Thus, you will never experience a sense of emptiness. You never confront the consequence of gaining ten pounds when you attempt to stop smoking, thus replacing one health issue with another. Instead, your overall health will improve in tandem with your sense of self.

We will utilize your body's propensity for forming new habits to combat your desire to smoke in a manner you have never experienced before. The portion of your brain responsible for quitting habits is feeble and easily distracted, whereas the portion responsible for forming habits is incredibly robust, as this is how the body increases its efficiency. It combines multiple duties into one, memorizes the process, and stores it in your background memory.

This is how we will win the struggle against smoking. We're going to begin by making a crucial adjustment. The reason most people fail to cease, and why you've likely failed in the past, is quite simple. You were attempting to refrain from doing something you desired.

Whenever I attempted to stop smoking in the past, a part of me always wished to continue. While 80% of me desired to quit, 20% of me missed the sensation, the sound, the ritual, and the first dose of nicotine into the bloodstream. That is precisely what hinders us.

I'm going to teach you how to supplant your craving for cigarettes with disgust. Now, smoking is an abhorrent and revolting practice for me. When I observe individuals smoking, I find it revolting. It has been so simple for me to resist the urge to return to smoking because I do not long for that cigarette.

Your Life After Retirement

The most beautiful part about quitting smoking is that your life immediately begins to change. Within fifteen minutes, the first health benefits will manifest.

It is a lengthy process, but you will eventually become stronger, faster, and more secure with your body. Breathing becomes marginally simpler. Regrettably, it is a lengthy procedure to regain complete and total health. It can take up to fifteen years to thoroughly recover from smoking, regardless of how long one has smoked. Therefore, it is imperative that we begin immediately, but please understand that you are not alone.

In 2015, the CDC conducted a survey and found that 68% of smokers desired to cease. This indicates that if you are in a room with nine other smokers, seven of you want to cease. This is the majority, but because we don't speak up, we believe everyone wishes to continue smoking.

Imagine "Future You"

Please take a moment to envision your possible future.

What is it like to not be a smoker? What does it feel like to no longer have control over your emotions and actions? How does it feel to no longer be a captive to an unpleasant habit? How does it feel to sense your life lengthening? Now, rather than pondering whether you'll retire in your fifties or sixties, you ponder whether you'll live to be a hundred or a hundred and twenty.

All the money you once spent on cigarettes and cigarette taxes can now be spent on other positive habits and pastimes, such as buying movie tickets or paying for your children's college education. Looking at the statistics, it is astounding how much we spend annually on cigarettes.

Imagine waking up every morning without coughing, without the need to light up a cigarette, and without the need to avoid smoking in your vehicle so as not to lower its resale value. Suddenly, when you wake up, the day is brighter. You are not breathless. You feel strong and energized as you descend the staircase, eager to seize life by the reins. You experience a sensation of liberation that has been absent for so long.

The home of How to Give Up Your Cigarette Habit

You will discover the exhilaration of quitting smoking in the following book. If you implement the information I'm about to share, you will discover a variety of incredible benefits:

Save cash. No longer should you fund companies that do not care about you and sell products that are steadily killing you.

Take charge of your wellbeing. No longer will you receive dirty looks from your doctor or be hesitant to attend your annual physical; instead, you will feel comfortable and confident with your body.

Stop smoking without worrying about acquiring weight. You will be able to eliminate and replace a bad habit without replacing it with another bad habit.

Stop feeling like a slave. You will no longer feel as though someone or something controls your daily decisions.

If you smoke because you are forced to or because you are addicted, cigarettes and tobacco control you. Breaking these constraints is incredibly liberating.

Enhance your physical conditioning. You will once again be able to run and ascend staircases without heavy breathing.

Regain your attractiveness. No more discolored teeth. No longer will you age and smell like stale nicotine.

Enhance your social standing. People will no longer perceive you negatively. No longer will children point to you in the presence of their parents.

Do these advantages sound like something you would like to experience? If this is the case, then let's discuss this book and how it can aid you on your voyage to quitting smoking.

About How to Give Up Your Cigarette Habit

This book is part of a series titled "Develop Good Habits," which I (Jonathan Green) co-authored with Steve "S.J." Scott.

Steve is a master of habits; he has extensive experience assisting others form (and break) habits. As he has never struggled with this type of addiction, he has never held a cigarette between his fingertips. Using a combination of his habit framework and my personal, practical experience with ceasing smoking, Steve and I decided to form a partnership.

Together, we aspire to facilitate your life transformation. We will share life experiences and our knowledge of how to solve various problems. Through our passion for assisting others in leading better lives, we will also share our personal experiences.

This book is about efficiency, and we know that you are extremely busy, so these pages will not contain a lot of filler or empty promises. Instead, we focus on providing you with vital information as efficiently as feasible. The purpose of this article is to simplify the process and get you started on the road to quitting smoking.

Moreover, many books provide a wealth of gold gems for enhancing one aspect of your life, but few explain how to incorporate it as a specific habit. They emphasize theory and why, but not how, which is a crucial aspect of ceasing smoking.

Those who succeed and those who fail are differentiated by the small actions they take in between their big ideals.

We will provide a step-by-step framework on how to better your life and produce a lasting result in the shortest amount of time possible. Our objective is to assist you in quitting smoking as quickly and painlessly as feasible.

By necessity, some of the information in this book will be duplicated in subsequent volumes. We've discovered that nearly all habits follow similar and repeatable steps, so we believe it's essential to provide a framework that can be used to create or break any habit.

That's enough for now.

Now is the time for action, so let's get down to business and transition from talking about quitting smoking to actually quitting.

Reflection Questions

Why did you choose to read this book?

Why did you initiate smoking to begin with?

What is the primary factor that keeps cigarettes in your hand?

Are you prepared to resign, or are you hesitating?

Are you prepared to increase your desire to cease from 80 percent to 100 percent?

How does an existence without the costs and curses of smoking make you feel on the inside?

Your Plan of Action

Tracking your progress is one of the best methods to accelerate your success in developing a new habit or modifying your behavior. Record your experience in a journal. This need not be anything extraordinary. It may be a notebook purchased at a local dollar store. On the front, type "Quit Smoking Journal."

In your journal, you will first respond to the reflection questions from the previous section. Next, compose an account of your life one year from now. Describe what it's like to wake up and walk outside in the morning without the need or desire for tobacco.

The greater the amount of detail used to paint this picture, the better.

How are you treated differently by others? How do you feel differently? What makes your experience unique?

Describe how extraordinary your life will be once you quit smoking. Join me in the following chapter, and we'll bring you one step closer to making your ambition a reality.

## Why You Ought To Stop Smoking

If you're a smoker, you've likely heard all the reasons why it's unhealthy to continue smoking and why you should quit as soon as possible. Whether you are quitting for personal or health reasons, it is essential to be aware of all the ways quitting smoking can benefit you and help you live a healthier life. This chapter will discuss some of the numerous reasons why you should quit smoking immediately.

Possible motivations for quitting smoking include the following:

According to a number of studies, those who smoke nicotine may find it difficult to concentrate on important aspects of their lives. Not only will the smoker have more trouble concentrating on simple tasks that they must perform at work or in their daily lives, but research has also shown that those who smoke will develop midlife dementia earlier and at a faster rate than those who do not smoke. Stop smoking as soon as possible if you want to have a clear head and avoid memory problems later in life.

May result in diabetesA study published in the Journal of the American Medical Association found that current smokers have a 44% greater risk of developing diabetes, particularly type 2 diabetes, than those who have never smoked. Those who smoke the most are at the greatest risk. In fact, an analysis of this case revealed that close to 12 percent of those who presently have diabetes developed it due to heavy smoking.

Since you've started smoking, have you observed that you're ill more frequently? Studies have shown that smokers have a significantly higher risk of contracting infections, particularly those caused by bacteria that cause pneumonia, compared to nonsmokers. In fact, the evidence is so compelling that the

Advisory Committee on Immunization Practice has recommended that all smokers aged 19 to 64 receive the pneumococcal vaccine. Many hypothesize that this is because the compounds in cigarette smoke may damage the respiratory mucous membranes. This will make it much simpler for pathogens to enter and cause disease. In addition, smoking may compromise the smoker's immunity, making it less likely that they will be able to deal with and combat any infections they acquire.

These problems with immunity and infections are not restricted to those who smoke. In fact, according to a study conducted and published in Tobacco Control, children who were exposed to secondhand smoke in the home as infants are much more likely to suffer from severe illnesses and wind up in the hospital during their childhoods.

Rather than spending a lot of money on pills and other methods to enhance and improve your sex life, you should consider quitting smoking. It has been demonstrated that smokers are much more likely to experience sexual issues than nonsmokers, and the more they smoke, the greater the risk.

Early wrinkles--are you concerned that your skin is starting to appear old and wish to regain its former youthful radiance? This is possible if you can quit smoking as quickly as feasible. A 2007 study published in the Archives of Dermatology found that smoking increases the likelihood of acquiring wrinkles on all areas of the body.

Acceleration of menopause - the menopause is a period that most women dread. They must cope with the issues of aging, inability to do many of the things they are accustomed to, and lack of procreation. Compared to nonsmokers, smokers may have to experience this at a significantly lower age. This occurs as a result of the fact that the chemicals in cigarettes destroy the egg cells in the ovaries. Menopause typically occurs when the number of reserved embryos falls below a certain threshold. All of this means that if you smoke for an extended period of time, more oocytes are destroyed and your body is signaled to enter an early menopause. Even if you have not yet experienced an early menopause, fertility issues can arise due to the same risks associated with smoking.

Vision problems are prevalent among chronic smokers. In fact, a 2006 analysis of 17 studies revealed that active smokers are at least twice as likely as nonsmokers to develop ocular diseases. Stop smoking immediately if you want to maintain your vision for an extended period of time.

Those who smoke have a greater chance of developing osteoporosis as they age compared to those who do not smoke. This is due to the fact that many of the compounds present in cigarettes can reduce the bone density of postmenopausal women, although the risk is high for both genders. In addition, if you are a smoker and you break a bone, you will experience significantly slower healing periods.

Some smokers report that regardless of how much sleep they get, they still wake up feeling sluggish. This may be due to the fact that smokers have a more difficult time falling asleep than nonsmokers, and it is believed that nicotine is the cause. The nicotine can disrupt sleep in two different ways. First, smoking makes it difficult for the smoker to fall slumber. Second, the smoker may experience withdrawal symptoms while sleeping. Both of these factors can make it difficult for a smoker to get the rest they need to feel refreshed the following day.

No one enjoys contemplating their own mortality, and everyone desires to live as long as possible. This is extremely unlikely to occur if you are a chronic smoker. In fact, according to a study published in the Archives of Internal Medicine, nonsmoking males live approximately ten years longer than their smoking counterparts. In addition, former nonsmokers will enjoy a vastly superior quality of life. If you want to live a lengthy life and remain healthy throughout those years, it is not beneficial to smoke for a few years.

Cancer has been associated with numerous types of cancer for a long time. This is not limited to the conventional conception of lunch cancer. In fact, the CDC has released a report estimating that 2 million of the cancer cases they received between 1999 and 2004 were caused by tobacco use. Cervical, bladder, urinary, kidney, pancreatic, stomach, bronchial, and lung malignancies are some of the cancers that fall under this category. If you want to reduce your risk of developing cancer, you should never start smoking and quit as soon as possible if you are already a smoker.

Alter your diet

Some individuals are accustomed to smoking after meals. This is their preferred behavior. The study demonstrates that certain consumables, such as meat, make cigarettes more satisfying. Others, such as vegetables, fruits, and cheese, make cigarettes taste awful. So incorporate some variety into your daily diet. Like exchange usual burger or steak for a veggie pizza instead.

If you are concerned about weight gain, you can replace cigarettes with sugar-free lollipops, sunflower seeds, gum, celery stalks, or carrots. You can also substitute nuts for cigarettes by consuming four nuts in their shells for each cigarette you wish to smoke. Thus, you use both your mouth and your hands and experience the same physical and oral sensations as when you smoke.

Keep yourself occupied

People often find it easiest to quit smoking on Mondays when they have school or work to keep them occupied. The greater your distraction, the less likely you are to desire cigarettes. In addition to being a good distraction, staying active helps you maintain a healthy weight and boosts your vitality.

Make your surroundings smoke-free.

Remove all cigarettes and tobacco products from your home. This includes not only cigarettes but also lighters, ashtrays, matches, and any other smoking-related products. In fact, you should make every effort to eliminate the odor of cigarettes from your home. This can help you quit smoking more quickly.

Prepare for the congestion

It is common for a smoker's congestion to worsen after quitting smoking. Many claim that this makes them feel worse for a period of time after quitting smoking and increases their temptation to resume smoking. Resist this enticement! Usually, the congestion gradually subsides.

Instead of smoking during work breaks, enjoy a video game on your computer.

Gaming is yet another addiction. It is more enjoyable and takes roughly the same amount of time. When you have a break from your work, consider playing computer games. Yes, some companies prohibit such activities, and then suggest an alternative 5-minute diversion, such as taking a walk, making a phone call, or eating a piece of fruit outdoors (but not in areas frequented by smokers).

Do not be frustrated by mistakes.

If you make a mistake, do not give up! It's conceivable. Major transformations frequently undergo false beginnings. If you are like many people, you may be able to cease smoking for weeks or even months before experiencing a craving so intense that you feel compelled to give in. Or perhaps you find yourself in one of your induce situations by accident and give in to temptation.

If you make a mistake, it does not indicate that you have failed. It simply indicates that you are mortal and capable of making mistakes. Here are three methods to get back on track:

Consider your lapse as a single error.

Determine when and why it occurred, then proceed.

Did you become a chain smoker after smoking a single cigarette?

Most likely not. It simply occurred incrementally over time. Remember that smoking one cigarette did not turn you into a smoker. Thus, consuming one or even two or three cigarettes after quitting does not constitute relapse.

Remind yourself why you're stopping and how well you've performed.

Include someone in your support group, family, or circle of friends who will perform this task for you.

Keep active through exercise

Keep active with activities such as running, walking, swimming, and stretching. A scientific study demonstrates that exercise reduces appetites and helps the brain produce anti-craving chemicals.

Be positive

Consider the positive. Keep in mind that you will feel better if you quit smoking. After a few weeks, your food will taste better and you will wheeze less. Whether you believe it or not, it is useful.

This optimistic outlook will assist you in staying on course.

You can also tell others that you do not smoke. This method will help you overcome your desire for cigarettes.

Reward yourself

Stopping smoking is not simple. You are deserving of a reward! Put aside the money you expend on cigarettes on a regular basis. When you have gone a week, two weeks, or a month without smoking, reward yourself with a movie, a gift card, or some new clothing. Celebrate this annually throughout the smoke-free years. Just remember that you have earned it by ceasing smoking.

Make non-smoking acquaintances

Spend your time at a function with those who do not smoke. Just remember that you should not covet smokers when you observe them. Make some non-smoking acquaintances. This is because when you are in the company of smokers, you begin smoking unconsciously. By staying with non-smoking companions, you can overcome your desire for cigarettes.

Do not permit smoking in your residence

This can increase your desire for cigarettes. Try to disregard it. You may place a modest "No Smoking" sign on your front door.

Switch to a botanical tea

Substitute a cup of medicinal tea for your cigarette habit. Preparing tea and sipping it slowly as it cools will provide the same pressure alleviation as a hit of nicotine. Or, try carrying cinnamon-flavored toothpicks with you and sucking on one each time a cigarette craving strikes.

Participate in athletics

You may participate in whatever athletics you desire. You can enjoy cricket, football, tennis, badminton, and other sports there. These activities will increase your physical activity and help you avoid smoking.

Determine when you have cigarette cravings

An urge can last up to five minutes. Before you quit, prepare a list of five-minute techniques. For instance, you can exit the party for a moment, converse with a non-smoking friend, or do anything else to avoid smoking.

Recognize that the first few days are the most difficult.

Especially if you intend to quit smoking, the initial few days are the most difficult. You will most likely feel despondent, irritable, exhausted, and sluggish. After effectively navigating the first few days, you will begin to feel normal.

Stop purchasing packs of cigarettes.

Please stop purchasing cartons of cigarettes and purchase only a single pack. You will eventually discover that when you want to smoke, you do not have any readily available. This will gradually reduce the number of cigarettes you smoke.

Participate in a new hobby with non-smoking companions.

Try a new pastime with your nonsmoking pals. This expedites the success that follows. When you are no longer a smoker, it may alter your perception of yourself. As much as you desire to quit smoking, you might be startled to experience sadness or longing for it. That is typical. Caution is warranted because, typically, a depressed mood will induce the desire to smoke.

Resist the urge to smoke while traveling or riding in a vehicle.

Remove the cigarettes, ashtray, and lighter from your vehicle and stock it with healthy treats such as sugar-free gum and hard candies. Sing alone while playing your preferred music. Maintain a clean vehicle and use deodorizers to eliminate the odor of tobacco.

Use Medication (Nicotine Replacement Therapy) - Chapter III

If you're looking for a relatively painless method to quit smoking, nicotine replacement therapy may be for you. This is typically done in conjunction with a physician, but there are also nicotine replacement therapy medications available without a prescription. Patches, gum, inhalers, lozenges, and even nasal spray are available.

Nicotine patches deliver a measured dose of nicotine through the skin and help you quit nicotine permanently in two weeks. A patch can be obtained without a prescription, and there are various strengths and types available for purchase. There are 16-hour patches and 24-hour patches available. The average or light smoker would choose the 16-hour nicotine patch because their nicotine dependence is lesser. Additionally, the adverse effects are less severe with this patch. The 24-hour patch is intended for heavy smokers, but it can cause adverse effects such as dizziness, rapid heartbeat, headache, nausea, skin irritation, and sleep disturbances. The amount of side effects you experience while using this patch will depend on the quantity of nicotine in the patch, the brand used, and the length of time the patch is worn. There are several things you can do if you are using a patch and experiencing these side effects, such as using a reduced dose or a different brand.

There is also nicotine mouthwash. Fast-acting nicotine gum is absorbed through the mucous membranes in the mouth. Like the patch, it is available without a prescription. You must ingest it until you experience a peppery taste or tingling, and then hold it in your cheek until the flavor disappears. When it does, you chew it again until the peppery flavor returns, then position it back in your cheek. It is suggested that you perform this activity for up to 30 minutes. It is recommended that you refrain from eating or drinking for approximately 15 minutes before and after chewing gum, as food and drink can influence its effectiveness. Similar to the patch, you will need to consider whether you are a mild, moderate, or heavy smoker. Then you can select the gum with the appropriate nicotine content. This also has some adverse effects, including mouth ulcers, nausea, jaw pain, throat irritation and an unpleasant taste.

Let's conclude by discussing the nicotine nasal spray. As nicotine is absorbed through the nostrils, this method is the quickest of all. This product, unlike the gel and the patch, requires a doctor's prescription. These sprays are beneficial for those experiencing withdrawal symptoms, as they effectively eliminate them. Be sure to adhere to the FDA's recommendations regarding the duration of use. Typically, no doctor will prescribe it for longer than three to six months. This has the adverse effects of a runny nose, watery eyes, coughing, sore throat, and sneezing. Clearly, the adverse effects are less severe than those of the gum and the patch. However, nasal sensitivities and asthma can be aggravated by the spray.

It's all about communicating with your physician and understanding what's best for you. There are numerous options available; therefore, you should research them and determine which ones perform.

www.ingramcontent.com/pod-product-compliance
Lightning Source LLC
Chambersburg PA
CBHW050029130526
44590CB00042B/2276